The National Poetry Series was established in 1978 to ensure the publication of five collections of poetry annually through five participating publishers. The Series has been funded over the years by Amazon Literary Partnership, the Gettinger Family Foundation, Bruce Gibney, HarperCollins Publishers, The Stephen and Tabitha King Foundation, Lannan Foundation, Newman's Own Foundation, Anna and Olafur Olafsson, Penguin Random House, the Poetry Foundation, Hawthornden Foundation, and the National Poetry Series Board of Directors.

THE NATIONAL POETRY SERIES WINNERS OF 2025 OPEN COMPETITION

Low Flying Planes by Hajjar Baban
Chosen by Jake Skeets for Milkweed Editions

Field of Vision by Stephanie Horvath
Chosen by Elisa Gonzalez for Penguin

Cloud Builder by Weston Morrow
Chosen by Ariana Benson for University of Georgia Press

Wildest by Kira Alexis Tucker
Chosen by Siwar Masannat for Akashic Books

Diary by Yi Wei
Chosen by Sasha Roque Pimentel for Beacon Press

Cloud Builder

Cloud Builder

POEMS BY WESTON MORROW

The University of Georgia Press
Athens

Published by the University of Georgia Press
Athens, Georgia 30602
www.ugapress.org

Designed by Melissa Buchanan
Set in LTC Goudy Oldstyle Pro
Printed and bound by Sheridan Books

Printed in the United States of America
30 29 28 27 26 P 5 4 3 2 1

EU Authorized Representative
Easy Access System Europe--Mustamäe tee 50, 10621 Tallinn, Estonia, gpsr.requests@easproject.com

Library of Congress Cataloging-in-Publication Data
Names: Morrow, Weston, 1991- author
Title: Cloud builder / poems by Weston Morrow.
Description: Athens : The University of Georgia Press, 2026. | Series: The National Poetry Series
Identifiers: LCCN 2026018887 | ISBN 9780820380674 paperback | ISBN 9780820378039 pdf | ISBN 9780820378022 epub
Subjects: LCGFT: Poetry
Classification: LCC PS3613.0778536 C56 2026
LC record available at https://lccn.loc.gov/2026018887

for Weston Morrow (1956–1972)

All men are created cloud builders. We exhale a stream of air that is warm and moisture-laden. The water in this expired breath will condense if cooled to the dew point. We do not always see our breath, but on winter mornings nothing is more common. . . .

Incidentally notice that when we cease cloud making we cease to live.

—Alexander McAdie (1863–1943), *A Cloud Atlas*

Contents

III

Cloud Builder

Skying

During his intense "skying" period, [John Constable] produced dozens of watercolor, crayon, and oil studies of the clouds over Hampstead Heath. . . . He labeled almost all of these images with scientific precision, indicating the date, time, wind, and weather conditions under which they were painted.

—Elizabeth E. Barker, The Metropolitan Museum of Art, 2004

It must have been owing to some nameless desire
to contain the aspects of our world

in every shape and iteration.
Or perhaps it stemmed from a need to hold

your breath before your face,
a shroud, a reminder

of your dying wife.
You knew it was impossible every time

you tried to set us down
on canvas. Even the dust

knows as much, that nothing remains
long enough to capture. Nonetheless,

you knelt, enraptured, at our feet
for hours, anointing them in oil,

fingers slick with cerulean
and linseed. But the wind needs

must have its say, thrusting us
across the plain

white fabric like a hand
brushing the eraser flot

from the page.
The devil drives us on,

Rothbart's swans, our bodies
always *en passé*, lifted

by a gust and spun. None of us
is what we seem. Though you call

something *sun* to bring
it down to earth,

it escapes.
At the end of the day,

the body is a cage
the soul falls back to,

the sky a stage
of grief we pass through

in search of horizon.

I

The Dead Won't Shut Up

Even gone they want
me to echo them

but standing
at his grave

I turn away
as from a stray dog

stop following me

what do I owe the dead
boy who gave

his name to me
like a coat left

discarded on the street
I never asked for this

to live my life
and his

for years
after my father draped

his dead brother's
name across my back

I thought I could return it

Pentiment

Repentance, remorse; a visible trace of a mistake or an earlier composition seen through later layers of paint on a canvas

Constable tried to paint the world he knew—
his neighbors, childhood friends
who stayed in Suffolk—like the River Stour
that wanders through *The Hay Wain* tries,

in murky reflection, to replicate the sky.
When I was young, a print of it hung above
the fireplace at the O'Bans' house. All that time
I failed to understand what it meant.

A wagon in a stream—big deal.
How could that mean as much
as the possibility Marie might kiss me
in the AMC 15 while the credits rolled

for *Garden State? And you stood at your door*
with your hands on my waist, the Dashboard
Confessional lyrics I planned to set
as my away message on AIM.

The past was dead, gone, and the future
would resemble the present. I thought
I saw where all of this was headed.
When I visited my friend, a decade later,

to apologize for my absence, I noticed the painting,
which hung there, still, waiting for me to see
the nostalgia blurred in each smudged leaf,
the past dissolved to nothing but impression.

Mrs. O'Ban told me parts of Stour Valley,
where Constable grew up, remain
almost unchanged from what he painted
two hundred years ago. And every day

that fact becomes less true. Even then
he was guessing, inventing it as he went.
Confined to London for his wife's
poor health, he had to paint *The Hay Wain*

from memory and ten-year-old sketches,
filling in the gaps lamp black.
If I look close enough at the lower third
I can just make out the shadow of a man

on horseback, obscured by the rising stream—
the artist, perhaps, who wanted to go back
so painted himself in, but changed his mind
when he saw he no longer fit.

The Double

It was my uncle's birthday.
We were meant to go place flowers
on his grave. But I was nine, and all I wanted
was to watch the Kingdome die

on TV—the implosion, building collapsing
into itself. Nothing grand about its end,
except maybe the dust,
whole clouds of it billowing up

to blot the midday sun, the remains
fanned out, cast in stone
like the fossilized hood
of some massive Cambrian jellyfish,

like a deflated circus tent, nostalgia
already rushing in to take its place.
I watch the demo now in reverse,
dome swelling like a popover,

sucking the billowing clouds of dust
inside, each row of blast caps
buttoning closed like a shirt, keep rewinding
past the beginning of the video—before

they scrapped the seats, peeled back the turf—
to '95, the Division Series, the Double, and Griffey
rounds home toward third, the ball leaves Edgar's bat,
drawn back to Jack McDowell's outstretched hand.

I don't believe it. It just continues, Niehaus screams
on the radio broadcast. It just continues, and I keep
rewinding, before I was born in '91, before the fall
in Berlin, before the wall even went up, before the bomb

tests in the desert, before the chain reaction
of the cancer cells, and the dust
that blew downwind into my uncle's lungs
is sucked back into the makeshift village at Trinity—

the proving grounds—where great men
like Oppenheimer and Fuchs tested
themselves against god at the expense
of children like my uncle. And so time

and time again we choose ourselves,
the feedback loop compounds, and history
repeats like the scratched CD
my sister plays in her room:

Stevie Nicks in "Silver Springs," stuttering:
Time—Time—Time—never quite reaching
the rest. So we sit, mesmerized by destruction.
Our fathers go to the grave alone.

The Aroma of Tacoma

I'm back for the first time in years,
so my dad drives me north, through Nalley Valley
and the once overwhelming stench
of brewing pickle fumes, past Tacoma Screw,
the pulp mills of my childhood spewing plumes
of steam into the sky: cloud machines
we called them, my brother and I, blaming the thick
gray altostratus sheets on their endless belching;
where once, on a walk, our dog slipped his leash
and disappeared into the trees, until, days later
he returned home, scratched and flea-bit,
following his nose. We keep going, down from Hilltop
to the Superfund site at Ruston, the town that copper built,
not a mile across, now a park and luxury apartments
stacked atop the slag heap; where the Silver Cloud
Hotel—*proudly smoke- and pet-free*—sprawling beached
on the shoreline, offers Copper River king,
delicately plated on a bed of fennel leaf and watercress
for fifty bucks a head; *refined dining,*
my dad says, laughing at his own joke;
where once, each night, the hacking cough
of lungers in their bunks rang clear
across the Sound to Vashon Island and Brown's Point,
where a young Frank Herbert watched
the smelters glow, imagining
a desert world choked and stinking
in the sand-laced fog of spice.
We park the car to walk the decontaminated beach,
the cool breeze of the marine layer tousling the reeds.
My dad shakes his head. *Beautiful, right?*
And it is beautiful, but I can't smell a thing.

Galloping Gertie

Narrows Bridge, Puget Sound (July 1–Nov. 7, 1940)

Oh, she could dance all right.
At night, high above the Narrows,
bathed in orange light of sodium vapor
lamps, she could bend and sway,
and all the boys would stop their cars and stare
at Gertie's smooth chassé—wind plucking
cables like a harp, whistling through
the guardrail gaps like teeth, like Otis Redding
sitting on the dock at Titlow Park, waiting
for the cymbal crash, the break
and fall to earth. It would come

four months after opening to traffic:
the spans collapsed, steel girders buckling
under the strain of harmonic flutter.
At the end, still just fifteen, my uncle
could barely lift his feet in bed, the cancer
spreading from his pancreas, the months
of chemo not enough to save him.
They gave him to my grandpa in a box.
Sometimes, when my father calls my name,
I wonder how he can bear to look at me
without a sense of loss, how he could stand
to say it as he laid me down inside
the stanchions of my crib. Above

the footage of the buckling bridge, a man
narrates, breathless, the collapse:
Tacoma will rebuild, he says. If you look out
across the water, you'll see two bridges now,

spanning the narrow band of Sound
where their predecessor lies in state,
chunks of rebar-studded concrete rising
from the beach like grave markers.
If you listen, you can hear the old song
of wind on steel, each of us dancing
up to, and beyond, the edge of ruin.

Boys of Summer

The boys lean forward, almost swaying
with the breeze, eager, if the ball should come
their way, to scrape their palms for it, to bleed.
They signal to each other—*heads up, eyes open*—

two fingers in the air, it's almost over.
Soon, there will be nothing left
but dirt, a little mound of earth
eroding, smothered in Scotch broom.

Fifty years go by. I find myself
standing, playing catch with my dad
on that same familiar plot, Douglas firs
skirting the outfield wall, stratocumulus

clouds unfurling like ink blots above
the flat gray roof of Interlake High School.
Eventually, then, a boy returned—the same
name but not the same body, that first one

dead in a Bellevue cancer ward and buried
in a cemetery I never saw. I came too late
to change all that. But still, at night his memories
come roaring back to me: how he burned

his way around the base paths, cursed
at every booted grounder, every fly ball
dying on the warning track. There was a time
he too would leap into the sky unhurt to catch

the fading light. I walk the diamond, then
scraping my shoe against the mound, begin to dig
as the day before my own surgeon did.
The line, four inches from my heart,

will scar, I hope, and hair will grow
above it, and like this place, the jagged
name my toe traces here in dirt, will fade.
Uncle Weston, I'm afraid that when I'm gone

no one will care. Will my whole life—
like yours—be reduced to words and buried
on an inside page of newsprint?
I tried to write my way to something lasting,

but I failed. I tried to win a game
that can't be won. Of all the things I touch,
only this patch of dirt, flecked with sun, remains.
Tomorrow, at a bar, I'll carve our name into a brick.

Cloud Study: Stratocumulus

The dead drag their souls across the sky
like Hefty® bags of trash, each cold black
lump of cloud its own malignant mole
pocking the back of Puget Sound;
and Mount Rainier, thirty miles south,
rises from the earth, a naked mound of scree,
carves a long, smooth gash through the side
of every passing cloud, and the dying grass
below grows stale on acid rain and leachate.
The decomposing corpse of Rainier, the man—
somewhere outside Sandwich, England—
swells like a too-full soda can and pops.
He never saw his eponym. Our bodies
erode in different intervals than rock.
The wind keeps blowing in our sleep, and
though the sky looks still from where we stand,
it carries on above. Meaning accrues, condenses
on a name. The sun tracks east to west,
and our shadows overtake us.

Rainstorm over the Sea,
John Constable, CA. 1824–1828

On the bluff above the beach, a faint green light
blinks and goes out. The fireflies come on:

first one, then five, then twenty, a whole night sky
of shifting constellations over the lawn—

Orion, Castor, Pollux, every ancient apparition
blazing just beyond our reach. He lifts his brush,

swipes in flat, wide streaks, the rain at Brighton Beach
falling in torrents over the Channel. This is why he paints

his loved ones in the stream, the sky, the quiet places
of the earth, clutching at a life that constantly evades him.

And maybe this is why I reanimate him now—to ask him how
to keep going in the face of illness, death. Around him

it grows darker. The storm is only worsening, and soon
he'll need to leave in case it turns to shore.

His strokes grow violent as the wind picks up
and his mind turns north, to his wife,

convalescing at the baths, sucking steam to fight
the growing pain of breathing. An insect flutters past

and without thinking he reaches out
and slaps it—sees the blood, the viscera,

luciferin unspool bright green
from the bug's thin carapace—a streak

of light, a momentary crack in darkness. In the future,
his successors will give up. A time will come,

in a hundred years—after Cézanne, Matisse, and Braque—
when we can no longer depict the figure without mutilating it.

Chiaroscuro

Italian; chiaro (clear, bright) + oscuro (dark); (1) contrast of light and shade; (2) partly revealed and partly veiled

Horizon falls away—
in all these landscapes,

far as the eye can see,
clouds descend in sheets

and stoop as fog to sweep
their bellies along the sweat-

soaked earth, and we
follow their lead. This

ecstatic grief—all
bodies bleed

together. Lacking
time, the painter

conjures life from shades
of darkness. This,

Goethe said, is whence
all color comes. The moment

runs. Rain clouds
raise the dust.

I feel you here beside me.
Come closer. Let me look at you.

Elegy with What Little Remains

I've been writing my father's obituary
since fifteen. To kill him, maybe, or save myself
some pain later on. Maybe it's a way of coping,

starting early. Still, it's hard
for a son to put his father in the ground
prematurely, have him burned,

reduced to ash and a few words—
a date of birth, a handful
of places he worked, and who survives;

much harder for a father to write one
for a son. They gave him six months,
my grandpa, to write my uncle's.

I imagine he waited, took his time,
prayed, in what little faith remained,
to a protestant god on whom

he'd soon give up. I imagine
my father, twelve, at home
with the babysitter, brother dying

down the road. My father still lives,
but I'm afraid each time I press
and flatten him on paper, he fades a bit.

Some details should stay between kin—
how it was at the end, how his skin
sagged in the sleeves of his letterman jacket,

the name of the cancer that killed him.
That's it. That's all you get.
He lived, and then he didn't.

The Jackalope

My grandpa Jack loved it. Because he loved everything
implausible. He, who while others slept, stole
from the house to disconnect the starter to my father's car.
No wonder he saw in this American trickster myth
a kindred spirit. He always blamed the cryptid
for his antics, told me stories of the beast
each time the TV's rabbit ears failed to reach
a signal through the static. Setting the antennae
on his head, he joked about the rabbit antlers
sprouting from his skull, said *impossible*
just means undiscovered. And when coyotes howled
through Chino Valley, he said *they're hunting*
for the Jackalope, but they'll never find him—the night
come alive with mystery, the mythic creature hiding
in every shadow. He said the Jackalope was bred
by god himself to outrun death—born mid-thunderclap.
In actual fact, though, its origins are far less magical.
At the height of the Depression, a taxidermist tossed
a dead rabbit on the floor, and when the corpse slid up
against a pair of pronghorn antlers, he mounted them.
But, to me, the truth is less important than the possibility
that, just beyond the limits of our vision, a whole world exists.
In the 1930s, pathologist Richard Shope began hearing tales
of Midwest rabbits with horn-like growths—
Papilloma virus, it turns out—tumors sprouting
from their heads in gnarled stumps.
This was a long time ago now,
when scientists scoffed at the belief
a virus could cause cancer. What they hadn't seen

couldn't possibly exist. When Jack began having headaches,
his doctors gave him aspirin and said they'd soon disappear.
And, eventually, they did. One night, after my parents left,
the Jackalope came and took my grandpa with him.
One last act of mischief. The man—vanished
in a blinding flash of lightning—become a myth.

Creation Myth

The story begins in the west
	of Texas, beneath an unforgiving sun,
with a widower and his children,

	three boys and a young daughter—
barely a toddler—the man's favorite,
	last reminder of his wife. In the story,

as my father tells it, she never gets
	a name. So when she eats the night-
shade, he says, *the young girl's death*

	drove the father mad with loss.
He dropped the three boys off next door
	and vanished. *The young girl, the father . . .*

this is how we talk about our own family
	history, as if recounting a fable.
Three generations back, our knowledge stops.

	This is not, right now, an indictment
of who receives a name, who doesn't.
	This is just a function of time, abandonment,

a catalog with half the items clipped.
	There is no one left to remember
the young girl's name, or her mother's.

	No one to remember how the brothers came
to Arizona, not exactly. I know the eldest son
	rode west, paid to bring his siblings out,

and raised them; that he raised their children too
    when the boys grew up and, like their dad,
couldn't handle the pain that loving someone brought.

    My grandpa Jack would speak of Uncle Ott
the way he used to speak, before his own son's death,
    of god. But no one talks about the others—

the father, the daughter, the younger brothers—
    except in family lore, the myth we tell of origin.
An all-consuming flood, or Saturn devouring his son,

    a little girl someone loved,
nameless, faceless, picking berries from a shrub:
    all shadows at the edge of fire.

Index of Refraction

She appears to me like this—in the rising smoke
of the fire pit, amid the scent of burnt oak and marshmallow,
enrobed in polyester housecoat like the Seamless Robe of Christ—
my grandmother. She sits, as she always did, cross-legged
in the sky blue Barcalounger, Betty Boop ashtray beside her.
In her hands, the cigarette and burnished gold
can of caffeine-free Coke glow like saintly attributes,
the backyard smelling almost, for a moment, of Clairol.
Then suddenly, with a change of wind, she's gone.

Atheists say every saintly visitation can be explained
by science, and I'm inclined to agree. Probably,
the smell of hairspray mixed with smoke
just triggered some sense memory, the floating tufts of ash
reminding me of her Vancouver apartment—
Mount St. Helens looming from the balcony. *See,*
she told me, *even saints can smoke. She's just letting off steam.*

In the moments following eruption, Mount St. Helens disappeared
within its own ash column—like *a thunderhead* or *a nuclear blast*
observers said. It turned the day to night, turned color shots
of Spokane black and white. The silicates, pumice, chlorine gas
erased horizon in one long, black exhalation.

Volcanologists track the spread of this expired breath
using the Index of Refraction, a metric
that includes both *real* and *imaginary* parts.

What is real and what's imagined? I can see the cigarette
delicately set between bent fingers. It glows red at the end,
ash sloughing to the pebbled glass of the drink stand

where it settles with the pollen of a ponderosa pine.
What's left behind defines us, my grandfather wrote me once.
We sift through layers of sediment to reconstruct a past,
a person, that exists now only in our minds. Real or imagined:

the pink silk bonnet she wore to protect her curls;
her voice calling me in for dinner with her dead son's name;
the swan-shaped jewelry box, neck ringed in pearls;
how she felt each time she called, and I was the one who came.

II

At the End of the Road

You have died. . . .
—*Colossians* 3:3
—*The Oregon Trail*

All my ghosts come back,
dying slowly, smoking cigarettes
and speaking French. Even the cats,
dead this past decade (hawk, car, diabetes),
have returned to sleep, curled up
in the crook of my knee. The coyotes
dad killed last winter tuck their chins
before the fireplace. Grandma, Grandpa,
Uncle Weston (cancer, cancer, cancer).
By grace, I have been saved
from dish duty, my mother
waving me over to the living room.
For the first time in years,
the whole family is here and
I'm remembering how to be happy,
outwardly, to see them.
My brother quotes Camus,
and mother doesn't like it, says it's morbid
to make light of death. But *c'est la vie.*
I leave them all downstairs, go up
to the computer room. I boot my old game
and watch the pixelated oxen
crawl across the screen, pulling me,
the wagon, all my tobacco
and ammunition, out the long and
treacherous path to Washington, the nineties.
I write the name of every dead family member
in my wagon, hit enter, try to see
how each of us will die this time.

Taking Bainbridge Ferry Home After a Funeral

The sticker peeling from the rail says, *Live*
with Porpoise. On the prow below, two men
in Patagonia half-zips vie for prime position,

inching forward in their quiet struggle
to be the first to disembark, like
a pair of seagulls eyeing the last flaccid

french fry on the surf-soaked deck.
Watching them compete, I'm reminded
of the Greeks arriving on the beach

at Troy, how Protesilaus shoved his comrades
sternward for the right to go first—
to trample Trojan sand, to wear

the crown of valor as the man
who led all others through the breach.
I used to find such acts of courage brash

or vain, but Protesilaus heard
the oracle proclaim: *The first to land*
will not come back. Still, he leapt.

I had no idea my friend was dying—
my friend who loved me, who asked
for nothing, and got that from me, in return,

who, at thirty-five, said everything
he'd ever say. Meanwhile, I cowered, afraid
every spot that marked my skin could be malignant.

Severe dysplasia, carcinoma in situ: nothing to fear,
the doctor said, but all I heard was cancer.
All I ever hear are signs of immanent disaster,

the symptoms of incurable disease
appearing as I read them.
I don't know what it means to face death bravely.

Yesterday, I watched them bury
the man who could have told me.
Doesn't he, too, deserve to stand, crowned

in sunset, beside me at the gunwale—
to smell the diesel in the salt air
burning? To look up,

to read the sign, portside, hallowed
as any ancient omen: *When You Ride*
Washington State Ferries, You Never Ride Alone.

The Cornfield,

John Constable, 1826

It opens on the countryside, a boy
who from a distance seems dead,
head tipped forward in the stream
as if drowned. Or is he looking

down, through the silt,
for something beneath
the surface? Surely,
there is nothing there
to see. No,

drawing closer it seems
he's only drinking
the dark water, slaking his thirst
before crossing Dedham Vale.
You think

this child might bring the scene to life;
meanwhile, in a bed, tucked between
Brighton and Hove, your wife is dying.

No one will buy this painting. To them
it is lifeless, even with the addition of the boy
and his dog, the little poppies blooming
on the hillside not yet reminders
of loss. The sheep march onward
to be shorn. The farmer hangs in his corn
a warning to the sparrows, a corpse
of cloth and stuffed straw.

But the birds know
what the man won't admit—
the body is a frail imitation
of its god, betrayed by every cough
of wind. Its small truths
riddled with fraud. What now
remains? The road persists,
but the village you claimed
you saw, beyond the lane,
never existed.

The House on Rowell Street

I am trying to remember
how the air smelled
in summer, how the light
fell across the apple tree
in the backyard, the old fence
covered in ivy, the mere
suggestion of a fence, really,
the ivy coating everything
in my memory like a film
of dust—the vines, the dark
leaves, the holdfasts like
fingers reaching in the dusk.

I am trying to remember
the sound at night.
Weren't the tree frogs
croaking? Weren't the owls
hooting softly from their snags?
There was a forest then, behind
the house, bracken lurking
at its edge, the fiddleheads
unfurling like secrets.

Didn't Quinn slip quietly
into my room to play
with Lego while I slept?
Didn't the TV whimper
through the night like a dog
begging to be let in?
The halls are smoke
and sunlight, floorboards
groaning from the strain.
There is too much here
to hold. Too much here
to save.

I Remember How It Was So Bright

Every day,
something amazing,

the ocean on fire, twice,
a boy falling out of the sky.

For years, I didn't know what it meant.
I pulled the sheet above my head,

pleading with the clouds to cover
the suffocating blue face of summer.

Somewhere else, men suffered,
withering in the sun's hot gaze.

Every life is a maze, though we seek escape
in different ways. Every morning

before I woke I felt the warmth on my cheek
of someone watching

over me, my father's hand, that fed
the stove while I slept, and then

came to carve me out of sleep,
brushing back my hair

like a dead leaf from the woodpile.
Bruegel painted it twice—the myth

of Icarus—man in flight, boy
falling, already underwater,

calling out to Daedalus,
drowning in his father's name.

I came home one day from school
and found my father sobbing

on the porch. I remember
how it was so bright.

I remember how he grabbed me
and held me there, how the tears

streamed down, hot
across his face, pouring

into his open mouth
so he sputtered, gasping for air.

I didn't want to watch
him drown—out of sympathy

or pride, I couldn't say—
unsure how to navigate

that space. A boy, afraid,
grows up—gulls wheeling

overhead, sun rising—and sets
his whole life on fire.

Leaving Lakewood

The first time I left someone I loved
I was seventeen, cleaning cum
off the fabric of a Volvo's backseat,
the parking lot of the Baptist church
behind the 7-Eleven and Sunny's
Market empty except for the teens
loitering and smoking blunts
rolled from grape Swisher Sweets.
I drove by again last night
on Google Maps, half naked,
squinting in the blue light
of the computer screen, clicking
methodically down Old Military Road
toward a memory I'd tried to forget.
I don't even remember why I left,
except, it must've been easier than staying.
Is this what counts for nostalgia now—
dropping pins on a road someone else
drove down, the persistent guilt of being
alive gnawing at the gut like hunger?
Nothing's changed.
It's all the same, but the grass
is dead in different places.

Birds of America

Plate 76, "Virginian Partridge"

The hawk diving, talon's
outstretched, into a flock
of quail, scatters them—chaos
then, a tangled mess
of wings and legs and as yet un-
snapped necks—animals
frozen in the act of death;
at least,
that's how Audubon depicts it;
how in *Guernica*, for instance,
the horse's head, the woman's
open mouth—the whole sick
mound of flesh—insists
our attempts to depict suffering
can never quite match
our ability to inflict it:
Picasso abusing his wife,
Audubon selling slaves
at each new port
as if a person's life
were nothing more than pigment, easel,
canvas: another plate
for the book.
We can never know
what happens after
the hawk descends
on the partridge nest.
Still, for some reason,
the raptor

seems just as shocked
as its prey. Isn't this the nature
of painting? The simultaneity
of suffering,
whole histories of violence pressed
to a single frame, blurring cause
and effect, reproduced without end.
How, when we were young,
my brother and I wrestled
in the yard, working ourselves
into a frenzy.
When, at last,
dad forced us apart,
I went to the basement
to play *Duck Hunt*, blast
each digital bird from the sky,
'til I was calm enough
to apologize
and hand my brother the gun.

The Galloping Ghost of the Pacific Coast

Dormant, rusting by the northern bank of Commencement Bay,
hull streaked brown, paint chipped and dulled gray,
more cockroach now than Silver Swan, the aging ferry
lists in shallow waves. Abandoned

by the city she loved, her famous eight-piece
orchestra gone, MV *Kalakala* goes down to her fate
quietly—no violin, no cello left to croon
"Nearer, My God, to Thee." But she was beautiful

once, admired. For thirty years, each day, she carried
sailors through the Sound between the shipyards and Seattle—
the same route I rode home drunk while my wife, still
a stranger, watched the ships float past the Fremont Bridge.

For thirty years, I failed to understand
the daily acts love requires—waking up
sober beside her, sorting the pill organizer,
making sure she eats. Too often I relied

on grand gestures—believed the myth
of the extraordinary: the rumors
of boaters on moonless pleasure cruises,
who've claimed to see beams of silver light

in boatless wake. Each time they get close,
it vanishes. But I return for this, to watch the ship
tugged slowly down Hylebos to her final berth,
where hydraulic grapples wait, arms extended,

to begin their work. I don't know what I expected
to see—the ancient workhorse, joints creaking,
buck, throw off her lines and flee? No. I tell myself she knew
where this was headed from the start.

It Starts with a Disaster

I.

The world turns from black and white to color,
but my uncle's fast asleep by then, in his hospital bed,
twenty minutes into the film, when the house swoops
down from the tornado into Munchkinland.
Standing in the doorway, Dorothy gasps.
For the first time, she sees the world, in fact, is beautiful.
But is it, really? At the end, we hear
from Auntie Em that Oz was just a dream.
We can see, on Dorothy's face, the hesitation.
Judy Garland turns chagrin into relief.
She's just happy to be home at last.
But there *is* no place like home for her, not now
that she's a star. She will never be herself again.
What they make of you is everything you are.
Her contemporary, the starlet Frances Farmer begged
fans later in her life, *I am the kind of person I am,*
and not a legend that arose.

II.

I steer between the lawns at Evergreen Washelli
Cemetery, searching for the spot. I have to navigate
by landmark: finding first the crying angel cenotaph,
foundation cracked from cedar roots and rain.
Rising from immaculate grass, it points the way,
by chance, to the ashes of my family, stacked
like bags of Quikrete in the columbarium wall:
Jack, Betty, Weston; brain, lungs, pancreas;
lion, scarecrow, tin man, marching

through the Emerald City gates to be made
whole. I dream of them, like Dorothy
imagining her Auntie Em while she naps
on her crimson bed of poppies, covered
in asbestos snow. Judy Garland doesn't know
yet, at sixteen, the damage carcinogens
could wreak. It wouldn't matter anyway—
the Seconal, prescribed to treat insomnia,
inducing respiratory depression while she slept
at forty-seven. She'd been on it since her teens,
drugged to sleep each night on set, awoken
hours later with amphetamines. At her funeral,
Ray Bolger, who played the Scarecrow, claimed,
She just plain wore out.

III.

It's better to burn out than fade away, wrote Kurt Cobain,
quoting Neil Young, in his suicide note. The year before,
he hung Christ on the cross in a field of red poppies
for the video to "Heart-Shaped Box."
He said he wrote the song for kids with terminal cancer.
That kid has heart, Dylan said, after hearing
Nirvana perform. A dangerous thing to have,
like contraband. It makes cowards afraid.
They chased me up to the castle of Aberdeen with torches,
just like the Frankenstein monster, Cobain told *Monk Magazine*.
I got away in a hot air balloon. He must've thought,
then, of Farmer, the *freak from West Seattle High*,
ostracized before her fame for her prizewinning essay
"God Dies." Her classmates, years later, must've reveled
in her fall from grace—the publicized conviction, reports

she took her milk mixed with Benzedrine and liquor.
She never did *have her revenge*, as Cobain predicted
in her eponymous song, dying instead
of esophageal cancer at the age of fifty-six.
She haunted him, though, and haunts me now too,
her faceless visage looming, erased by the public gaze.
At the end of her life, she said she understood,
finally, *the power and meaning of the Crucifixion.*

IV.

There comes a point, Farmer said, *when a dream*
becomes reality and reality becomes a dream.
How she screamed, for instance, at the judge
who sentenced her to Western State—
the psych ward abutting the park
where I grew up, the soccer fields
and baseball diamonds where my coaches
tried, and failed, to teach me to be brave.
I remember once, when I jumped for a header
and collided with a friend, how the ground fell away
and the clouds above me spun like pies
in the display case at the front of Spiffy's diner,
how afraid I was. I never leapt like that again.
And I am still afraid today, scalpel poised
above my chest, though the surgeon says
it's all routine. There comes a point where fear
supplants the truth. I think of Farmer planting crops
with other detainees where, now, people walk their dogs
and browse the farmer's market booths,
the Technicolor park desaturating as she passes
through the doorway to her cell.

V.

I knew nothing, then, of pain.
What my uncle must've felt, dying at fifteen.
Jack and Betty splitting in his wake.
According to the ancient Greeks, the gods
set humans in the sky, as constellations, to alleviate
their suffering. I have tried to do the same,
scattered them like stars upon the page,
and in the process robbed them.
In the end, it's Dorothy's grief
that earns her entry to the Wizard's hall.
Can her companions not see
it's loss, most of all, that makes us human?
When it's done, the Wizard floats away in his balloon,
Garland shouting from below, *Come back!*
After sentencing, Farmer asked the judge
for that one thing she lacked—regard.
As the bailiffs hauled her, struggling, from the room,
she screamed, *Have you ever had a broken heart?*

The Cloud

Nothing's ever really gone, mom told me
when, at twelve, I started using the internet.
She meant *be careful what you post.* I don't
think she meant to speculate about the nature
of the self, the soul, whether we live
on as ghosts or echoes in the minds
of friends, but she was right. Shelley wrote

of clouds, *I change, but I cannot die,*
and all this life's detritus I store online—
old passwords, chat logs, pictures of my dick—
remains, invincible in its stillness, like the shepherds
in Poussin's *Arcadia.* Now I find myself

scrolling through iCloud, ten years since
we broke up, and suddenly she's here,
my ex, naked, in the room before me,
legs splayed across our bedsheets—

fingers frozen, blurred, in motion—thighs
pale as a plucked bird's—face locked
in ecstasy—faked, surely, for the camera.
I realize I'm not breathing, as if the picture knows
neither one of us should be here.

In the redshift light of my phone screen, her body
half-turned away from me, she seems
almost shy, as if the woman in the picture
no longer recognizes my face. What I'm nostalgic for
is gone, or, more likely, never existed. By the time
she sent this, she'd already left me

in her mind. She'll never know I held her here
so long, selfish, like a hoarder.
She's not the ghost; it's me who haunts
the past, who can't stop turning back
for one last look. All that's left to do—
all I can give her now—is reach out and delete it.

III

Long-Distance Aubade

The mules outside are braying
the coarse, keened prelude
to our morning drive. Parting

the blinds, I can see them—
hemmed in by their wooden pen,
drunk on rotten pears, carousing

in the rising steam of their own breath.
The Airbnb, which used to be a shed
I think, is freezing. Your bare feet,

frigid, envelope mine, and cursing,
I turn toward you, stick my hands
on your back to make you squirm.

It's still early. We have hours left
before checkout, but the sun
is up, the sound of mules intruding

on the dawn, and both our calendars
are booked through Easter. I remove
my hands to find my phone,

to search for spring flights to Ohio,
check the miles left in my account.
The mules are prancing now,

throwing back their heads—two dumb
and stomping lovers, tilting at the fence,
drunk on wild, ignorant desire.

Weymouth Bay with Approaching Storm,
John Constable, 1818

Maria Constable (1788–1828)

The unobstructed view, nothing in our way
now, finally, Maria—this empty beach,
our future reaching through the distance

out of frame. There's a village there, a country house,
a family behind the clouds. Seven kids. God knows I wish
I could tell you they live on forever. But look,

John-Charles and Emily will soon meet you on the beach.
Keep walking, step from the boat and let the air
of the windswept coast whip hard across your face.

Maria, we had some good years, didn't we?
After all that waiting, the tide, at last, drawn
back to give the sand its say. But even here,

in my own painting, I can't hold time at bay
forever. All my life *I have been running after pictures,*
and seeking the truth at second hand. I am done with that.

Remember that first night on the banks
of the Stour, as your father talked
to Reverend Rhudde, and behind his back

you held my gaze? I saw then, in your eyes,
something more than all I'd sought
in the Old Masters. When you coughed

clouded bile on the shore of Brighton, I knew
I'd spend the rest of my life trying to capture
this moment, here, on the beach with you.

A Summerland

The sun tried to kill me. They cut a hole
        in my chest, pulled
                the lump of self-
    replicating flesh from the skin above my heart.

I had always thought I was invincible.
        When I set my wings and leapt
                from the labyrinth wall
    I was only following the men who made me,

men like my great grandfather, great uncles,
        men who tried,
                each in his own way,
    to escape. I make myself this myth

again so I can hide inside it. Until recently,
        I'd never been afraid
                no one needed me;
    I feared how I might act if someone did.

When my wife got sick what scared me
        was my selfishness.
                Let me go back
    to myth. When Icarus fell it was spring,

Williams says, because Bruegel put him there,
        amid the hawthorn branches
                climbing for the light.
    But if I could pick him up, restore him to the sky,

this time in Constable's *Ploughing Scene in Suffolk,*
        where the green
                pigment's faded
    so the trees seem dead, and the men

appear to dress the field as morticians might,
        he'd take comfort
                in its lack of sun,
    the clouds providing shade for him to hide.

But I can't bring them back to life—the boy,
        the man, his wife.
                I leave them all behind
    in the field where they've been planted.

Constable would have hated me
        inviting Icarus here.
                He refused
    to paint the mythic figures favored by his peers—

the histories, as well, great men like Hannibal or Nelson.
        He chose, instead,
                the ploughmen,
    told his friend, *I should paint my own places best.*

He meant the meadow, not the sickbed
        of his wife on Hampstead
                Heath. But I don't think
    he painted nature while she suffered to avoid

the truth. He knew, as Maria wrote him once,

We have many painful trials
required of us in this life,
and we must learn to bear them. A former title says

A Summerland—a reminder, perhaps, to himself:
This is the life that love
has given you.
Try your best to make it beautiful.

Weymouth Bay: Bowleaze Cove and Jordon Hill,
John Constable, 1816

Then let me beg and entreat that you will cease to think of me, forget that you have ever known me, and I will willingly resign even all pretensions to your regard. . . .
—*Maria Bicknell, letter to John Constable during courtship*

In the version without her,
everything is lighter. The clouds,
white and weightless, float

without a care—filled, still,
with their small, translucent
drops, unconcerned with loss,

the sand on the beach still warm
from the sun. There is a single man
standing at the berm, where the strand

gives way to vegetation.
He is waiting his turn. He is looking
for something in the water.

Though the tide continues ebbing,
forever, there's only the illusion
of movement. The plume

of smoke transmuted into placid sheep,
the iceless river frozen in its reach,
the man, too, reduced to scenery.

The Art of Letting Go

The acetone takes its time erasing the painting.
        I can no longer stand
to see it—the thin figure
        fading like a sun-
blanched awning, framed on the easel's
        narrow wooden legs.
How much longer now,
        'til the canvas gives up
the face, the cramped and slender limbs?
        While I wait I trace
across your back the strokes I'll make
        to lay the body down
on canvas, again. It's been so long
        since I touched you
idly, without intent, that my desire,
        swelling like a storm-spurred tide,
terrifies me. My hand quivers
        and the lines serrate,
jagged and misshapen, hooked
        like a crooked spine
to your hips. Our last attempt
        arrived lifeless.
Just a few more minutes
        and the solvent
will have finished the job, erased
        another failure. Each time
I make this same mistake
        of hoping, but eventually
we learn our lessons, and soon

I'll stop trying
to change the painting, let the space
between us bloom
into something resembling a life.

It Was About Regret

Does that make sense?
It was about filling one space
with something else. The sky,
for instance, filled with clouds,
the artist fighting time. Beyond
this frame—a little town, a life
I more or less imagined.

Runner

In spite of what we say, fog doesn't descend
on the city; instead, it rises from the ground,
the sweat from Earth's long labor, turning as it does
each day, like the breath of joggers taking laps around
the civil twilit lake. Or so I, who can't see
even six feet beyond my face, assume.
My exhalations mingling with the mist
to shroud the sycamores, the dogwoods
blooming out of view, the ornamental pear tree's
scent of spunk wafting to my nostrils on the dew.
Every morning they come—the joggers—
before dawn, the start of work,
as predictable in their movements
as the stars fading, one-by-one, above us.
You don't know I'm here. I left a note that said
I'd gone in early to the office. If you asked me why I lied,
I'd say something opaque like *I just needed to clear my head,*
the easy language of evasion. *All men,*
Alexander McAdie said, *are created cloud builders.*
And our current understanding of atoms tells us,
technically, to say we ever touched is false.
Though I have reached, again,
the parking lot, returned to where I started,
I don't stop. I push on—another loop,
and another, as if I could keep this up forever.

Jack & Betty

They held each other in the cold
white light of the cancer ward,

then, slowly, in the growing
silence, separated. Sometimes

there is nothing left to say.
Some failures have no lesson.

Their remaining kids grew up,
got married, had kids of their own,

alternated homes on Christmas, Easter.
Decades pass like that—memories

condensing on a moment, like vapor
on a mote of dust. They carried on,

as we must—the boy between them
diminishing, diminishing.

Possession

We don our jerseys for the game, the same player's name stamped across our backs.

We take it. Make it our own. Turn Cucho from man to symbol.

As a child, I struggled to understand the difference between love and possession.

I confused the stakes of life with games.

Even now, as I watch the players find each other in the gaps between defenders, I wish I could inhabit them, take the field.

Before kickoff, we stand with twenty thousand others in the afternoon sun and chant a dead man's lyrics: *Take my hand, Take my whole life too*—our voices joining the rest, rebounding through the bleachers.

At the thirty minute mark, I explain how fouls are determined by the ref, how the difference between yellow and red is often a matter of intent.

When we're up two-nil at half, you ask if we can leave.

The flares ignited in the Nordecke burn your eyes, the headache that you've nursed all summer worsening.

I say it's fine, and you know I'm lying.

I hold your hand the whole walk home, arms low between us, as if there were a gap to cross, as if we were distinct, as if my life belonged only to me.

Juncture

It's been abandoned my whole life—
though it used to be a street like all the rest,
connecting Frederick to Short—asphalt crumbling
back to dirt, crabgrass filling in the cracks. At ten,
I held Katrina's hand as we passed between brambles,

coming out the homeward side detached. And that first kiss
of a joint to my lips, the wisp of smoke curling
between the fingertips of Douglas firs,
happened in the space of that blind curve.

It remains just as it was, just empty enough
to set twenty years inside it.
And the rusted water tower, looming, still speaks
in faded red spray paint, *Gus was here*.
Our dog trots circles in the dust
as I tell my wife this place, to me, is sacred.

She asks, *Did you know him? Gus?*
I have no idea who he was,
or what his statement asks of us. And the pathetic
vessel that he chose to hold his name,
could it really ever serve as his stand-in?

There were times I felt unworthy of my life,
like I had stopped, and everyone I loved
kept moving on around me. I didn't want to die,
because I didn't think I'd done enough.

Already, I'm forgetting how it felt.
The dog cuts short his orbit, whines.
He sniffs the air, excited, as if he senses
someone there beside him. Like me, he wants
to remember everything. He considers digging
between patches of gravel, looking for god

knows what, but changes his mind. He turns away
to the rusted pipe that used to be a flagpole,
lifts his good leg, and lets the urine
dribble down the side—*I was here. Come find me.*

Ars Poetica

It is thus in all the fine arts. A new Gothic building, or a new missal, is in reality little less absurd than a new ruin.
—John Constable, lecture at the Literary and Scientific Institution, Hampstead, July 25, 1836

Not the sonnet.
Not the ode.
Not the cold turn

of celestial bodies
locked in orbit
of the same sun.

Even the comet
that appears just once
every eighty years

remains caught in the dust
of its old forms, the mad pursuit
of meaning, Athena born again

from the same sick head.
In a corner booth
of an empty dive bar,

the oracle at Delphi
still churns through
the same rote lines,

smoking cigarettes
and eating french fries,
wiping grease on her thighs.

Someone arranged
the constellations
in a distant time,

a location
inaccessible to us.
Old medallions, stamped

with the emperor's mug, lose
then gain, then lose again
their value. It's only matter

of perception. The moon tugs
at the ocean's hem each night
like a child seeking attention.

You cannot go back.
The past is gone.
You carried it away inside you.

One Final Time, Before His Heart Gives Out, John Constable Considers the Sky

March 31, 1837

I raged, Lord, believe me.
I raked my fists against the bars
of my cage—this body
you made me—and howled.

I screamed into that dark
hole in the ground
'til I was hoarse and tore out
what little I had left of hair.

I tried to fight, once. I chased the sun
down beneath the dirt and rose
again, empty handed, a burning red
effigy—Orpheus turning,

in every song, his dead
lover's suffering to art. I'm sick
of rage, God. I gave it all I had, got
nothing back. I accept that

now. The light is dying, and the children
are in bed. I'll finish these notes
on chiaroscuro in the morning.

Ship Burial

The dead kitten in a box, on the corner
of Livingston and Champion, two blocks
from East Columbus Veterinary Hospital,
we thought, at first, was sleeping.

We passed by you, pausing for a moment, like
mourners at a wake. The open casket
of your shoebox soaked by rain. My ancestors,
in Norway, buried those they loved—

their kinsman and their kings—inside
their burning ships, hastened them toward afterlife.
Though, damp, your box would never light.
I feel a certain guilt each time I name the dead,

as if I speak you back from slumber,
confused, to a world of strife. Reclaimed,
you come, recycled like the plastic tabs
my own cat, Nikita, hoards; the little yogurt jars

in which my wife plants starter seeds
each spring; or the ancient Greeks'
trim-ankled god Nike, whose name means
victory, who at Olympia, Pausanias writes,

sits cupped in the hand of Zeus
like a coronation orb or kitten,
and who now, in turn, cradles your still-
warm corpse in cardboard palms.

Was it the driver, or some later passerby,
who picked you up from cold concrete
and set you here, on Champion,
in the vessel of a god?

Hereafter

Was the sun better left
unhemmed, not yet

draped across
this flesh, decaying

into text? The night slipped quiet
through my fingers, and the light scattered

through my frame. I waded
through dusk, or maybe

dawn, predecessors hung
over my shoulders

like a mourning shawl.
At times, that cloth was all

the protection I could muster.
I wove my soul into the seams

of these moth-bitten
garments, this patchwork

verse. What dragged me, ragged,
back to the earth? A hole

in the ground, my whole
life, converted to dirt.

I was still waiting, then,
for something to happen.

As if action were inevitable, and time
flowed like a river, when it ebbs

like the tide. I still believe
there's a place out there

where past and future meet. See—
I hold it out to you.

Acknowledgments

The Adroit Journal, "The Aroma of Tacoma," "The Double," and "Creation Myth"
Atlanta Review, "Elegy with What Little Remains"
Barrelhouse, "The Jackalope"
Boulevard, "The Cloud" and "Leaving Lakewood"
Diode Poetry Journal, "Boys of Summer"
The Journal, "I Remember How It Was So Bright"
Lake Effect, "Skying" and "*The Cornfield*, John Constable, 1826" (originally published as "It Opens")
Meridian, "Hereafter"
Poetry Northwest, "*Birds of America*"
Redivider, "At the End of the Road"
Superstition Review, "The Art of Letting Go" and "The Dead Won't Shut Up"

This book is dedicated to Elissa Washuta, my wife and my first and best reader, who has held my hand through every difficult step of this process, who kept me going every time I considered giving up. This book, *and everything*, is for you.

To my family, especially my parents, Warren and Nancy, whose love and unwavering support made all of this possible to begin with. I am proud to be your son. To Sandra and Quinn, Daniel and Lucas, Wayne and Janice Morrow, the Rodríguezes, the entire Barich clan, Judy Snider, and those who are no longer with us: Weston Morrow, Betty Swann Morrow, and Jack and Helen Morrow. And to Neal Snider, who lit the spark in me and kept the fire burning, who passed away one month before the acceptance of this book.

To Ariana Benson, for selecting this manuscript, for your incredible generosity. I truly cannot express the depth of my gratitude.

To Isaac Willis, whose feedback has drawn me back, always, to the path; Liz Harms, for being my fiercest advocate and brilliant friend; Chris Vanjonack, for all the late nights and early mornings sitting on the floor trading drafts, and for helping me see the beauty in the world; and Zach Simon, for reminding me that poetry, like life, is meant to be enjoyed.

To everyone at the University of Illinois Urbana–Champaign who workshopped early drafts of some of these poems and made the five-hour drive each week feel like coming home: Claire Christoff, Drew Buxton, Madeline Furlong, Carrie Johnson, Deon Robinson, Chelsea Hill, Ali Shuger, Cole Piedimonte, Erich Slimak, and Matty Fash.

To Maya Jewell Zeller for things uncountable—and for treating me with kindness when I first wandered, foolish and naïve, into your office. To Janice N. Harrington, for teaching me to strive always to become a better poet today than I was yesterday. To Ángel García, for teaching me to be vulnerable. To Corey Van Landingham, for teaching me that beneath all the theory there's an actual world. And to Christopher Kempf, for teaching me that this labor of love is still a labor.

To John Dudek, Amy Hassinger, Ted Sanders, Jodee Stanley, Alex Shakar, David Wright Faladé, Kristi McDuffie, Dana Kinzy, Amanda Bales, Jordan Sellers.

To everyone at Central Washington University, especially Gary Bartlett, Cynthia Mitchell, Ryan Hopkins, Rhonda Muller, Krislon Rhynes, Katharine Whitcomb, Dan Martin, Josh Welsh, M. Eliatamby-O'Brien, Lisa Norris, Christopher Schedler, Matthew Altman, and Cynthia Coe.

To all my coworkers at *The Observer*, OPR, the *Central Kitsap Reporter*, *Fairbanks Daily News-Miner*, and to the warehouse team at TFA and everyone at Mount Cross.

To everyone at Ohio State, especially Marcus Jackson, Nick White, Lee Martin, Amber Blaeser-Wardzala, Allison Pitinii Davis, Kathy Fagan, and Michelle Herman.

To everyone whose advice aided the creation of this book, especially Victoria C. Flanagan, Eloisa Amezcua, Brian Tierney, Taneum Bambrick, Sharma Shields, Laura Read, Ellen Welcker, Kristen Millares Young, and Brian McGackin.

And to everyone whose support, encouragement, and friendship has made this life worth living, especially Elizabeth Redinius, Erin Corneliussen Mason, Sam Friedman, Lauren Frisch, Matt Acuña Buxton, Chanda File, Joe and Nicolien Buholzer Fox, Holly Seiler, Corey Burdick, Chelan Lippincott, Atticus Wallace, Frana BA, Leslee Caul, Kerry O'Connor, Eva Holland, Rod Boyce, Tania Clucas, Christian Torimino, Jessie VanMersbergen, Leslie Guild Kelly, Kevan Moore, Trey Howard, Kirsten Reach, Eugene Rutigliano, Ruth Awad, Eric Shonkwiler, Madeline Barnett, Anna Bressi, Amber Garriott, Kelsey Topolski, and Landan, Laurie, and Steve O'Ban.

To the Greater Columbus Arts Council for providing support that made the submission of this manuscript possible.

To all of these and many others—from the bottom of my heart, *thank you.*

Notes

"The Double" takes its name from the most famous hit in Seattle Mariners franchise history. In the 1995 Division Series game five, down one in extra innings, with Joey Cora on third and Ken Griffey Jr. on first, Edgar Martínez hit a walk-off double off Yankees pitcher Jack McDowell, winning the series and advancing the Mariners to the Championship Series for the first and only* time in franchise history. The hit is widely regarded as a major contributor to saving the franchise, as ownership had discussed moving the largely unsuccessful team to a larger market prior to the 1995 season. It is also cited as a major contributor to the franchise receiving funds from the city of Seattle to fund the creation of a new baseball stadium, thus leading to the demolition of the Kingdome in March of 2000.

The original Tacoma Narrows Bridge (at the time the third longest suspension bridge in the world) was nicknamed "Galloping Gertie" because of its tendency to undulate in the high winds that funneled through the Narrows.

The final line of "*Rainstorm over the Sea*, John Constable, CA. 1824–1828" is the author's iteration on a quote by Mark Rothko regarding the abstract expressionist movement: "a time came when none of us could use the figure without mutilating it."

The epigraph for "Chiaroscuro" is drawn from the *Oxford English Dictionary*.

* During the publication process of this book, the Mariners reached the ALCS for a second time—thirty years after the first—falling one run short of reaching their first World Series.

Constable painted *The Cornfield* in 1826 from his studio in London at a time when he was struggling financially. To this end, Constable added elements to the painting that he hoped would make it more enticing to buyers. In a letter to Rev. John Fisher, he wrote, "I do hope to sell this present picture—as it has certainly got a little more eye-salve than I usually give them." According to the National Gallery in London, the "eye-salve" in question likely referred to such elements as "the drinking boy, the donkeys grazing the bank dotted with poppies and cow parsley, the flock of sheep, distant village and meandering river." The final line of the poem is a direct quote of Constable's son Charles, who stated after the painter's death that, although much of *The Cornfield* is drawn directly from sketches Constable had done of Fen Lane in Dedham Vale, the village depicted in the distance "never existed."

The italics across the first two stanzas of "I Remember How It Was So Bright," are a line, split in half, from W.H. Auden's poem "Musée des Beaux Arts," which, similarly, is an ekphrasis of Bruegel's *Landscape with the Fall of Icarus.*

The Puget Sound Navigation Company often referred to the *MV Kalakala* (the star of its fleet of ferries) as the "Silver Swan," though locals allegedly referred to the vessel by other nicknames, like "The Galloping Ghost of the Pacific Coast" or "*Kackerlacka*" (Swedish for "cockroach") by the large Scandinavian population in the area. The metal-plated, silver-painted, art deco ferry captivated locals and visitors alike during the 1962 Seattle World's Fair.

In "It Starts with a Disaster," the italicized line, "*have her revenge on Seattle*" refers to the Nirvana song, written by Kurt Cobain, "Frances Farmer Will Have Her Revenge on Seattle." The quote, "*I am the kind of person I am, and not a legend that arose,*" comes from Farmer's appearance on Ralph Edwards' TV show *This is Your Life* a decade after her highly publicized psychiatric incarceration. Her quote, "*There comes a point when a dream becomes reality and reality becomes a dream*" is from a 1983 article in *The Indianapolis Star*, published thirteen years after her death. The phrase "*the freak from West Seattle High*" is Farmer's own description of how people in Seattle saw her. Recounting a publicity trip to Seattle that MGM executives sent her on early in her career, she told *Collier's* magazine, "What the Goldwyn people had forgotten was that up that way I'm still remembered as the freak from West Seattle High."

The line "*I have been running after pictures, and seeking the truth at second hand*" is a quote from a letter written by John Constable to John Dunthorne on May 29, 1802.

In "A Summerland," the line "when Icarus fell it was spring" comes from William Carlos Williams' poem "Landscape with the Fall of Icarus," which, like Auden's poem, performs ekphrasis of Bruegel's painting of the same name.

The quote "*I should paint my own places best,*" was written by John Constable to his friend Rev. John Fisher.

The quote "*We have many painful trials required of us in this life, and we must learn to bear them*" was written by Maria Bicknell Constable to John Constable during their seven-year courtship. The courtship was especially lengthy—and at the time of writing seemed doomed—because Maria's grandfather (her family's main benefactor), Rev. Dr. Durand Rhudde disapproved of Constable as a suitor due to his lack of prospects as a struggling artist.

The final line of "Hereafter" is an homage to the eight-line fragment "This Living Hand" by John Keats, written in December 1819 while the poet was dying of tuberculosis, just a few years before Maria Constable likely contracted the same disease that would, nine years later, kill her as well.